# The Universe Inside You

A Journey of Self-Discovery and
Spirituality for Children

**This Book Belongs to:**

_______________________

_______________________

# **Dedication**

I dedicate this book to my 6 beautiful children, who I love so much. Thank you for choosing me as your mother. Most of my lessons and growth during my lifetime, I've experienced through the years of motherhood. I am so tremendously proud of each and every one of you for the beings that you are. Continue to Shine your Lights and let your Love be felt wherever you are.

Thank you to my husband for always being supportive in everything I do and encouraging me to be the woman I am. You are my rock, my best friend, my soulmate. Love you.

Sarah

Dear readers,

I want to start by thanking you for choosing yourself in reading this book, my heart is full of gratitude for All of you.

Welcome to " The Universe Inside You", a special book that explores the spiritual side of life. In the pages that follow, you will discover ideas and concepts that can help you better connect with the world around you and find a deeper sense of meaning and purpose.

Whether you're just curious or you simply enjoy reflecting on big questions about life, this book is for you.

As you read, you'll learn about things like mindfulness, gratitude, kindness, compassion, the law of attraction, and how these concepts can help you live a more fulfilling life.

Above all, this book is all about embracing the beauty and wonders of life. So come along on this journey and see where it takes you!

As as a thank you gift for purchasing this book, I want to offer you The Empowered Child activity book. It's a Free Download that you can print out and follow along as you read this book. Get it here with the link below:
www.livelovelight.co/empowered-child-activity-book

**SPIRITUALITY**

Let's explore what spirituality means. Spirituality is a way of understanding and connecting to something greater than ourselves. Some people call this connection to something bigger than ourselves; God, the Universe, Source, Creator, Spirit and sometimes other different terms.

Spirituality is a way of finding more meaning and purpose in our lives beyond just the physical world we can see and touch. Spirituality is not necessarily about any specific religion, but rather a way of Life.

It can be experienced through different practices like meditation, prayer, acts of kindness, spending time in nature and many other ways.

You get to decide what spiritual practices feel right for you.

Throughout our time together, I will share some ideas that you can try out in your daily life.

**What does Spirituality mean to you?**

**GOD**

For the longest time, I thought that God was a man with a big white beard. Funny, right? To my surprise much later in life, I learned that it was not the case.

God is not a person like you and me. God is an energy that can be found everywhere and in everything. It's a bit like adding food coloring to water - God's energy is present in every part of the Universe, even if we can't see it or touch it.

God is not a physical being like you and me, but rather a consciousness that is present in all things.

What does consciousness mean?

Consciousness is a big word that describes something very important- it's what makes you aware of the world around you and the things that you're doing. When you are conscious, you know that you exist, and that you're a living being. Consciousness is what makes you YOU.

If God can be explained in just one word it would be LOVE.

Although we often refer to God as he or him, it's important to know that God is not male or female. God is an Energy.

Some people call him Creator, Source, Universe, but all these names actually mean the same thing. This Energy (God) is always present. We all hold a part of this energy within us and we are always supported by God. You are never alone.

To connect to God, Source, The Universe, however you choose to call this Energy, you can pray. Praying is communicating, it's like talking to a friend that you can't see, but that is always listening to you and who loves and cares for you. You can do it out loud or in silence. You can pray to say thank you, ask for forgiveness, ask for help and guidance. There are really no rules, you get to decide.

The Creator is also helped by angels and spirit guides who help you navigate your life.

**What does God mean to you?**

**How do you call this Energy that surrounds us?**

**YOU ARE A GIFT**

You are truly **Unique.**

There is no one on Earth that is just like you, which is why comparing yourself to others is not worth it, because we are all so different. Just Be yourself!

**You are a true masterpiece!**

What is a masterpiece you ask?

A masterpiece is an extraordinary Creation that is so Special and Valuable, just like YOU.

I once read in a book that we are the ones who chose to come here on Earth. I really feel that's true. We choose the parents we have as well as our siblings to help us learn and grow and experience life.

Along with God , you planned the right moment to come to Earth where you get to have so much fun and learn so many things.

You came on Earth with a mission and a purpose and you came fully equipped with so many unique talents to share with the world around you.

As you grow up, you will discover more talents, and gifts you have and how you decide to serve others with what you came here to share.

Do you want to know something else? You are so incredibly loved beyond words can ever be expressed. Even if sometimes you may not always feel that way, remember that God, your Angels and so many other Beings love you soooo much.

Take a minute. Give yourself a pat on the back and a big hug and tell yourself: " Good Job, I Love You, Thank you for being so amazing." You truly deserve it!

**What are some talents you have?**

**YOU ARE MORE THAN A BODY**

We are spiritual beings living in a physical bodies, which means there is a part of us beyond just our physical body. Our spiritual part is the part of us that thinks, feels, dreams. It's what makes us who we are as a unique person. Where as your physical being is your body that you can see and touch and that you use to move and play.

We live in a physical world that we experience through our 5 senses; touch, taste, smell, hearing and sight. The spiritual part of us, we cannot see it or touch it, but it's our connection to something more than us. Our spiritual side last forever. We can call this part Spirit or Soul, it's like a special energy that helps us feel more love, happiness and other emotions. This is the part of you that makes you so special and unique.

When we say that we are spiritual beings living in a physical body, it means that we are more than just what we look like on the outside.

## LOVING ALL OF YOU

Your body is like your vehicle that drives you through all your life experiences, which is why you have to take good care of it. You only have one physical body throughout this lifetime so it's important to treat it with love, care and respect.

Here are some ways to take care of your body;

**Exercise daily**
30 minutes of daily exercise can help you feel more strong and happy.

**Eat Healthy**
Eating food that nourishes all the cells of your body like fruits and veggies especially help you stay strong and energized.

**Take care of your physical body**
Showering and brushing your teeth shows your body that you love and respect it.

**Sleep & Relaxation**
It's important to give your body the rest it needs to be able to function well everyday.

**Love and accept all parts of you**
Say to yourself loving words. You can look yourself
in the mirror and say "I love you".

**Have Fun**
Taking time to play, dance & laugh are essential to
live a happy life.


**What are things you love about yourself?**

**What are things you do to care for yourself?**

## CHAKRAS

Chakra is a Sanskrit (spoken language in India) word that means "wheel".

Chakras are energy centers in our bodies that help us stay healthy and balanced. They are not visible, but they are present in our bodies.

You can think of your body as a house with 7 rooms. Each room has a special purpose, just like each chakra has a specific role in our body. Each chakra has a color and a feeling associated to it.

There are many chakras, but we will be covering the 7 main chakras that are in your body.

**Root**
Location: Sits at the bottom of your back
Color associated to this chakra: Red
This chakra is about feeling safe & secure

**Sacral**
Location: Sits just below your belly button
Color associated to this chakra: Orange
This chakra is about expressing emotions & creativity

## Solar plexus

Location: Sits above your belly button
Color associated to this chakra: Yellow
This chakra is about confidence & strength

## Heart

Location: Sits in the middle of your chest
Color associated to this chakra: Green
This chakra is about love

## Throat

Location: Sits at your neck (throat)
Color associated to this chakra: Blue
This chakra is about communication & self-expression

## Third Eye

Location: Sits between your eyebrows
Color associated to this chakra: Indigo
This chakra is about intuition & imagination

## Crown

Location: Sits at the top of your head
Color associated to this chakra: White
This chakra is about connection to divine

To keep your chakras healthy and balanced you need to eat good foods, sleep well and feel good. You can also practice yoga and meditation.

**Without any help, can you remember where all the chakras are?**

## INTUITION

Intuition is a feeling you get when you know something to be true, even if you can't explain why. It's like a little voice inside you that guides you. Your intuition is your inner knowing, a sense of what feels right for you in this now moment. Some people say they have a gut feeling, this feeling that you just know. You can sometimes feel it in your stomach too.

Have you ever felt like something was a good or bad idea, even if you didn't know why? That is intuition. It's a way of knowing something that comes from deep inside you.

To be able to listen more to that little voice, you need to become aware of it. You need to trust it and trust yourself and you need to act on your intuition, your inner guidance. The more you do, the more you will hear that little voice.

**Do you remember a time when you heard that little voice inside you? Did you listen to it?**

## YOU CO-CREATE YOUR LIFE

Have you ever heard the saying: "you create your own luck"?

Co-creating your life means you're like a superhero with the power to create the life and world you want by using your thoughts, words, feelings, and actions.

Imagine wanting to learn to ride a bike. Just wishing won't magically make you a pro rider. To create the reality of biking, you've got to take action. You could ask grown-ups for help or start with training wheels. You might wobble or feel a bit frustrated, but if you keep going, you'll soon be able to ride smoothly on your own!

It's totally up to you to decide what kind of world you want to make by how you think, talk, feel, and act. You're the artist of your own amazing life!

This is why it's important to plant what you want in your mind. Your mind is like a garden and your thoughts are like seeds, whatever you plant in your mind will blossom. Which is why it's important to plant positive thoughts.

**What do you want to create in your life?**

**What goals do you want to achieve?**

## YOUR THOUGHTS ARE POWERFUL

Did you know we have about 65 000 thoughts each and every single day. We have all sorts of thoughts that can be positive, negative or neutral. Most thoughts come to us naturally without us even realizing we are thinking about something.

The more you become aware of your thoughts, the more you have control over them and the easier it is to replace a bad thought with a more positive thought that feels good.

Your feelings are a great indicator to help you know when you are thinking positive or when you are thinking negative thoughts. When you are feeling bad, you are most likely having negative thoughts and when you are feeling good, you are most likely having positive thoughts.

**Do you think you have more positive or more negative thoughts in your day?**

**What thoughts do you pay the most attention to?**

**YOUR WORDS ARE POWERFUL**

Just like your thoughts, your words are also powerful. Words have energy and power with the ability to motivate, encourage, help, and heal. Words can also hurt and humiliate. Everything you say is energy and affects yourself and others around you.

Can you remember a time when someone gave you a compliment and how it made you feel?
Now, can you remember a time when someone said something hurtful to you and how that made you feel?

It's important to choose well the words you speak, because once the words are out of your mouth you cannot take them back. When you speak in a negative way try re-saying what you want in a more positive way.

For example:

Negative words
I can't do this, it's too hard.
I don't like the gift I received.
VS
Positive words
The more I try,the better I get.
I'm grateful for the people who think of me.


**Take a moment to think about some negative words you may have been speaking and transform them into positive words.**


**Try this:**

1. Take 2 seeds of the same type and from the same pack.
2. Plant them in 2 different containers, write A & B on the different containers.
3. Place the containers in the same place, give them the same amount of water and sunlight.
4. Now to one container you will say kind and loving words like: "you are so beautiful, you are growing so fast and strong, I'm so proud of you."

To the other container, you will say mean words like: "you are ugly, you are awful, nobody likes you."
5.  Repeat this Daily and Observe how your plants grow.
6.  Take notes of your observation.
7. Share with Family and Friends your observations on the power of words and how your plants grew.

## YOUR ACTIONS ARE POWERFUL

Your actions are what you choose to do and what will move you towards your goals and dreams. Remember when we said that you co-create your life and in order to learn to ride a bike, for example, you actually have to do something, right? You can't just wish and hope to ride without doing anything.

What's important is to take one step at a time to achieve whatever goal you have. Even the smallest step is meaningful to help the Universe bring you what you want.

It doesn't matter if you don't know How to do or get something, the important thing is to try. The more you take action steps, the closer you will get to what you want. The more positive actions you take the more positive your life will be!

## LAW OF ATTRACTION

There are many laws in the Universe. You may have heard of the law of gravity which is the idea that objects are attracted to each other because of their size and distance. It's what makes things fall to the ground. If you drop a book, it will fall straight to the ground.

Another amazing law of the Universe is the Law of Attraction that says that the thoughts and feelings you put out into the world can attract similar things back to you.

It's kind of like a magnet that attracts things that are made of metal. Your thoughts, your words, how you feel and act are like the magnet, and the things that come into your life are like the metal objects that are attracted to the magnet.

For example, if you focus on positive thoughts and feelings, you can attract positive experiences and people into your life. On the other hand, if you focus on negative thoughts and feelings, you may attract negative experiences and people.

What's important to remember is that you create your life and you attract into your life everything, which is why if you want good things to come into your life, it's important to focus on positive thoughts, feelings and actions.

Here is the process to attract what you want in your life:

1. **Know what you want**. Before you can start attracting what you want, you need to be clear about it. Write down your dreams, be specific.

2. **Believe that you can have it**. You need to believe that your desires are possible and that you deserve them.

3. **Imagine it.** Visualization is a powerful tool for manifesting your desires. Imagine yourself already having what you want. Focus on how happy and excited you'd feel.

4. **Take action.** The law of attraction needs action on your part to make the magic come true.

5. **Let it go.** Let your desires come to you. Have confidence that it is already on it's way. Let go of any worries or doubts that are holding you back.

6. **Say thank you.** Remember to be grateful for everything you already have in your life.

7. **Stay open.** Be open to receive what you want knowing you are deserving of all your dreams.

Remember, the law of attraction is not magic, it requires patience, consistency, and you have to use positive thoughts, words, feelings and actions on a daily basis.

To help you bring your dreams to life, try making a vision board! It's like a collage where you can put pictures and words that represent all the awesome things you want to attract in your life.

**Do you remember attracting something in your life without knowing that it was the law of attraction at work?**

**Try this:**

Create a Vision Board. Take a piece of paper and cut out in magazines or print images and words of what you would like to attract in your life. Then stick them on your vision board and look at it morning and night with the feeling that it's already in your life.

## RAISING YOUR VIBRATION

In order to create a happy life and feel good it's important to have a positive mindset.

One way to have a positive mind is to raise your vibration to a frequency that can attract positive things in your life.


What is a vibration?

Every living thing on this planet releases energy. Your inner vibration is the energy you put out into the world around you attracting like energy back to you, just like we talked about with the law of attraction.

This is why it's important to surround yourself with people and places that have good energy.

There will be times in your life where you won't always be joyful and positive and that's OK. Sometimes people can be unpleasant or we experience situation that make us feel negative thus lowering our vibration.

It's important to feel your emotions, but once you do, you can let go of the negative feelings and switch back your energy to a more positive energy.

Here a 7 ways to Raise your vibration:

1. Practice Gratitude. Appreciate the good things in your life to help you feel more happy and positive.

2. Go outside to play and be in nature.

3. Have a dance party.

4. Make silly faces with your parents, friends, or siblings.

5. Do an activity that you enjoy like coloring, building legos, or something that makes you feel good.

6. Ask for a hug from someone you love.

7. Notice 10 things around you that are beautiful.

**What do you like to do to Raise your Vibration?**

## YOU ONLY HAVE CONTROL OVER YOURSELF

In life there are times when we have control over things and other times that we don't. Like when your teacher assigns a project at school. Everyone in the class has to do it, including you. Even if you're feeling upset or frustrated, the project still needs to be done. Although you do not have control over the fact that you have a project to do, the important part is that YOU can control how you respond to it. Instead of being upset about it, you can make it more fun. Turn on the music while you are doing the project, imagine yourself doing a fantastic job, and think about all the new things you are learning. Same project, but two different ways of reacting can lead to two different outcomes.

THINGS
OUTSIDE MY CONTROL

THINGS
INSIDE MY CONTROL

How I decide to react to something

The weather

Other people's
thoughts

Other
people's
words

Others
behaviours

My behaviors

My thoughts

My words

My happiness

My Ideas

Other
people's
actions

My actions

My attitude

How other
people
treat me

Other
people's
happiness

Other
people's
attitudes

## GOING THROUGH BIG EMOTIONS

Understanding that you can only control yourself is a big step. But what about those times when an emotion sticks around longer than you want it to? Feeling sad, angry, or frustrated at times is okay, but it's important to handle these emotions in a healthy way.

Remember, you're the only one in charge of making yourself truly feel better.

Here is what you can do when you feel a big emotion like anger, frustration, sadness come over you:

1.  Recognize how you are feeling.
2.  Name the feeling that you have.
3.  Notice where in your body you feel it.
4.  Pause & Relax.
5.  Take a deep breath and let it out slowly.
6.  Use strategies that work for you to calm down; you can move your body, write about how you feel in your journal, squeeze a squishy ball, talk to someone you trust, draw a picture.
7.  Find a solution if there is a problem to solve.
8.  Ask someone you love and trust to help you if needed.

**What are some ways that help you calm down when you are feeling big emotions?**

**THE POWER OF NOW**

The present is a gift.

Living in the moment can be tricky because there are so many things trying to grab our attention. But here's the secret: the present moment is the only time happening right now. The past is done, and tomorrow (the future) isn't here yet.

Sometimes, when you think about a field trip or a big school presentation, you might feel worried. But guess what? Lots of the things we worry about often times never actually happen. That's why staying in the present moment is the most joyful thing you can do for yourself.

Mindfulness is a practice that reminds you to pay attention to the present moment without judgement. It helps you become aware of your thoughts, feelings, and physical sensations in the moment. This helps you feel more calm and focused.

Here are ways to help you keep yourself in the present moment and not let your thoughts wander:

✧ Focus on what you are doing now. For example if you are reading a book, focus on the book in front of you and that's it.

✧ Breathe deeply. Take a few deep breaths and focus on breathing.

✧ Avoid distractions on phones and tablets.

✧ Enjoy the present moment.

## MEDITATION

Meditation is a practice of training your mind to focus on the present moment. It involves sitting still, or laying down and breathing deeply. It helps you become more calm and relaxed. It can also help you concentrate better.

To meditate you can just stay quiet and let your thoughts drift away, you can put meditation music on to help relax yourself, you can repeat a mantra like I AM LOVE or you can also put a guided meditation.

Here are steps to get started:

✧ Find a quiet place
✧ Sit down comfortably with your spine straight or you can also lay down
✧ Close your eyes
✧ Take a few deep breaths, inhaling through your nose and exhaling through your mouth
✧ Focus on your breath
✧ If your mind starts to wander, gently bring your focus back to your breath

- ✧ You can meditate a few minutes or as long as you like
- ✧ When you are finished, take a deep breath and slowly open your eyes

Remember that meditation takes practice, the more you practice the easier it will become just like anything else.

## GRATITUDE

Gratitude is the practice of recognizing and appreciating the good things in our lives. It involves focusing on what we have rather than what we don't have, and expressing appreciation for the people, experiences, and things in our lives.

As we talked about earlier, gratitude means showing your appreciation. You have so many things to be grateful for each and every day; the food you eat, the home you have, the eyes that help you see. Sometimes we forget to see all these things that we have in our lives. The more you are grateful for what you already have in your life, the more the Universe will help bring you more to be grateful for.

You can keep a gratitude journal to write down all that you are grateful for each and everyday. You can also express it by showing your appreciation through kind words or acts of kindness.

Remember the more you are grateful for what you already have in your life right now, the more things you will have to be grateful for.

**Try This:**

Create your own gratitude journal.
You can decorate it however you like.
Everyday write at least 5 things that you are grateful for and really feel it.
Watch what happens!

## KINDNESS AND COMPASSION

Kindness and Compassion are important qualities that involve showing concern and care for yourself and others.

Kindness is the act of being nice and doing thoughtful or helpful things.

Compassion involves feeling empathy and understanding towards others who may be experiencing difficulties.

These qualities help build positive relationships, enhance well-being, and create more caring and supportive communities. Small acts of kindness such as helping a friend with their homework or giving someone a compliment can go a long way.

**What acts of kindness do you like to give and receive?**

**What acts of kindness do you do for yourself?**

**FORGIVENESS**

Forgiveness is the act of letting go of anger, resentment, or negative feelings towards someone or a situation that has hurt you. It involves choosing to release negative emotions and choosing to move on from the hurt caused by someone else.

When we forgive we let go of this negative feeling inside of us and we leave space for more positive emotions.

Forgiveness is not about saying what the other person did to you was okay, it's about letting yourself be in peace, moving on and letting love back in.

**Write out Who you feel you need to forgive?**

**Do you need to forgive yourself for things?**

## AFFIRMATIONS

Affirmations are positive statements that you say to yourself to help you feel good about yourself and your abilities. When you say affirmations regularly, it can help you build confidence, feel happier, and achieve your goals.

For more impact repeat your affirmations when you wake up and before going to bed.

Here are some examples of affirmations that you can use:

I am strong
I am healthy
I am smart
I am loved and valued
I am worthy of kindness and respect


**Now it's your turn.**
**Write affirmations that inspire you and repeat them daily.**

Remember: Affirmations are positive
          Affirmations are said in the present
          Affirmations usually start by I AM

# GROUNDING

Grounding also known as Earthing, is a way to connect with the Earth. It's like giving the Earth a big hug!

You know how when you walk barefoot on grass or sand, you feel good? That's because your body is connecting with the Earth's energy. The Earth has a lot of good energy that can make us feel more happy and healthy.

When we take off our shoes and walk barefoot outside, we can feel the Earth's energy. We can also connect with the Earth by touching trees, sitting on the ground, or even hugging a tree! Grounding is good for our bodies, because it can help us be more calm, improve our sleep, and even help us feel more balanced.

The next time you go outside, try taking off your shoes and socks and feeling the earth beneath your feet. You might be surprised at how good it feels!

## CREATE YOUR MAGIC MORNING

Have you ever heard the saying: "The way you start your day, determines the way your day will go."?

When you begin your morning in an intentional and positive way, the rest of your day will go better.

Starting your day positively is important to feel more happy, energized and ready to learn and play.

Here is how you can start your day:

- ✧ Wake up & Smile
- ✧ Think of things that make you happy
- ✧ Make your bed
- ✧ Get dressed and ready to start your day
- ✧ Move your body
- ✧ Eat a healthy breakfast
- ✧ Say your affirmations
- ✧ Read a positive book
- ✧ Visualize and Decide to have a good day

In the evening:

✧ Write in your gratitude journal
✧ Meditate and Relax
✧ Get ready for bed
✧ Repeat positive affirmations


**Try this:**

Create your Magic Morning ritual and see how much better your day goes.

**END NOTE**

During our time together, we've explored various ideas and concepts that can help you develop and better understand yourself and the world around you.
Through the different topics we covered in this book, it's my hope that it inspired you to connect to something bigger than yourself and for you to continue to be curious about spirituality and create your own practices.

Here are a few things for you to remember and share with others:

- ❖ We are all connected in this beautiful world.
- ❖ We are One.
- ❖ Be the change you want to see in others.
- ❖ Failures are just lessons and opportunities
  for you to improve.
- ❖ You are Unique and Amazing in your own way.
- ❖ You are Always supported.
- ❖ Everything is always working out for you.
- ❖ You have everything within you to live a happy life.


Let your Light Shine Bright and show the whole
Universe how incredibly special you are.

With Love & Light,
Sarah

As a thank you gift for purchasing this book, I want to offer you "The Empowered Child" activity book.
It's a Free Download you can print out.
Get it here with the link below:
www.livelovelight.co/empowered-child-activity-book

If you wish to go further on your quest, we invite you to join us in the fun course we created just for you.

You can join here;
www.livelovelight.co

Connect with us on Facebook at livelovelight and on Instagram at livelovelight.co

# <u>Notes</u>

# <u>Notes</u>